DISCOVERY GLOBE

Leon Gray

illustrated by Sarah Edmonds

CANDLEWICK PRESS

Copyright © 2017 by Quarto Children's Books Ltd.

Text by Leon Gray
Illustrations by Sarah Edmonds

First U.S. edition 2018

Library of Congress Catalog Card Number pending
ISBN 978-0-7636-9748-8

HHO 22 21 20 19 18 17
10 9 8 7 6 5 4 3 2 1

Printed in Shenzhen, Guangdong, China

This book was typeset in Gill Sans.
The illustrations were created digitally.

Candlewick Press
99 Dover Street
Somerville, Massachusetts 02144

visit us at www.candlewick.com

The Quarto Team
Designers: Duck Egg Blue and Mike Henson
Editors: Matthew Morgan and Nancy Dickmann
Creative Director: David Bennett
Associate Publisher: Jonathan Gilbert
Publisher: Zeta Jones

CONTENTS

YOUR GLOBE AND WORLD EXPLORER'S GUIDE

Discover the amazing diversity of life on planet Earth with your globe and World Explorer's Guide. Find out about the natural world and human history in your guide, then explore countries and continents with your spinning model globe. Using your globe, you can search for icons, answer questions, and get to know our incredible planet.

YOUR GLOBE

Follow the instructions on pages 6–7 and construct your globe. Then your discoveries can begin!

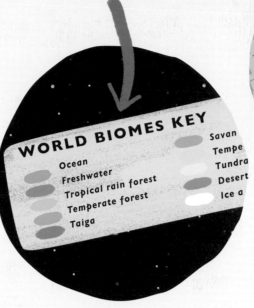

A key on the base of the globe indicates these different areas.

WORLD BIOMES KEY

Ocean
Freshwater
Tropical rain forest
Temperate forest
Taiga

Savan...
Tempe...
Tundr...
Desert...
Ice a...

Different types of land, such as savannas, rain forests, and deserts, are marked with colors on your globe. You can find the key for these on page 15 and the base of the globe.

You can also find different countries' borders, as well as icons that relate to topics covered in the guide, such as natural wonders and famous faces.

WORLD EXPLORER'S GUIDE

Your World Explorer's Guide includes different sections that explain Earth's place in the universe, the natural world, and human life.

QUESTIONS

Answer the questions in the book by referring to the globe. You can check your answers on page 46.

Why is Earth known as the blue planet? What are biomes? Which animal goes on the longest migration? What are some of the unusual jobs that humans do? Find out in your guide!

BIOMES

A biome is a large region with a specific type of **climate** and distinctive plants. Biomes such as deserts are found on land. Other biomes are found in water. Each is home to different types of animals.

The Amazon is the world's largest rain forest. High up in the treetops, animals from snakes to sloths make their homes in the maze of leaves and branches.

TAIGA

The taiga is a huge forest of evergreen trees that stretches across the northernmost part of Earth's surface. It is blanketed in snow for much of the year.

Huge portions of Russia, the world's largest country, are covered in taiga. Can you find two other countries with this biome?

ICE AND SNOW

Can you imagine living in a place that's colder than the inside of your freezer? The polar regions of Earth surround the North and South Poles, and only a very few species can survive there.

The southern ice cap is on land, in Antarctica. The northern ice cap is on water. In which ocean is it located?

DESERT

Deserts receive little or no rainfall. Few animals and plants can survive in them.

The Tuareg people travel through the Sahara, the largest hot desert in the world, to trade goods. Can you find which continent the Sahara is in?

TROPICAL RAIN FOREST

It's hot and humid in the rain forest. Tall trees form a dense **canopy** that blocks out sunlight and prevents it from reaching the forest floor. Rain forests cover just 6 percent of Earth's surface, but they are home to a huge range of different living things.

Looking at your globe, can you find the rain forest in South America?

ALL THE BIOMES
These colors are used to show the different biomes on your globe. Can you find them all?

Ocean
Freshwater
Tropical rain forest
Temperate forest
Taiga

Savanna
Temperate grassland
Tundra
Desert
Ice and snow

FRESHWATER

Freshwater accounts for less than 3 percent of the water on Earth. It is carried from one area to another by rivers, which flow through the landscape. Along the way, rivers give life to many plants and animals.

The Nile, in Africa, is the longest river in the world. Which sea does it empty into?

ICONS

Look for an icon by each entry to find the subject on the globe.

If you're not sure what something means, just look it up! Words shown in bold text, **like this,** are explained in the glossary on page 47.

ASSEMBLE YOUR GLOBE

To assemble your globe, you just need to slot together the cardboard pieces stored in the box that comes with this book.

Each piece is labeled on the back: N for Northern Hemisphere pieces, S for Southern Hemisphere pieces. NI is for the Arctic Circle, and SI is for the Antarctic Circle.

Remove the cardboard sheets from the box that comes with this book. Carefully press out the globe pieces, making sure you don't tear the tabs.

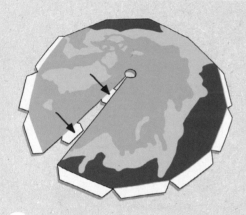

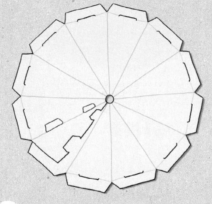

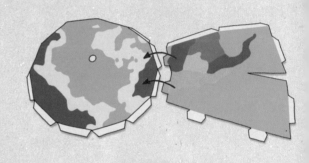

1 Fold the Arctic Circle piece along the creases and around the central hole. Insert the tabs through the slots.

2 Once slotted through, the tabs will hold in place to form a circular disk.

3 Take a Northern Hemisphere piece and line up the artwork on the Arctic Circle disk.

4 Push the tabs from the sheet into the slots in the disk.

5 Take the next Northern Hemisphere piece, line up the artwork, and insert the tabs into the circular disk.

6 Attach all the Northern Hemisphere pieces until you have a flower shape.

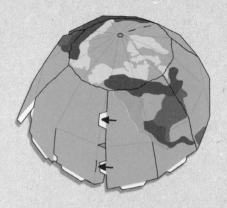 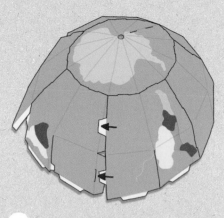 

7 Connect each Northern Hemisphere piece to the next, slotting the tabs into place.

8 Repeat the same process for the Southern Hemisphere.

9 Push the two wooden dowels into the connector to make the axis that the globe will spin on.

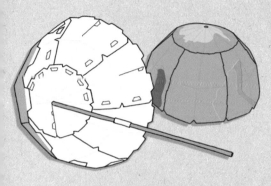 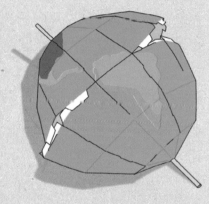 

10 Push one end of the axis through the hole in the top of the Arctic.

11 Slide the Southern Hemisphere over the other end of the axis.

12 Insert the tabs of the Northern Hemisphere into the slots in the Southern Hemisphere.

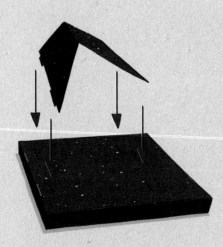  

13 Fold the stand in half and insert it into the box that held your globe pieces. It now forms the base for your globe.

14 Slide the axis into the stand and down into the base. Now you can start to explore!

EARTH IN SPACE

Earth is just one small planet in our giant solar system — the group of planets and other space objects that move around the Sun. Although our planet might seem big, it is tiny in comparison to the Sun.

THE SOLAR SYSTEM

Our solar system includes all the objects that move around our Sun: planets like Earth, and smaller objects such as **meteors, asteroids,** and moons. There are eight planets in our solar system and millions of smaller objects.

Mercury

Venus

Earth

Mars

Jupiter

Saturn

Uranus

Neptune

Note: these planets are not shown exactly to scale.

THE SUN

The Sun is a star — a giant ball of gas and plasma that **radiates** light out into space. Light from the Sun illuminates our days and keeps us warm. The Sun is approximately 93,000,000 miles (150,000,000 kilometers) away — about 11,500 Earths could line up side by side in that distance! If your globe and the Sun were to scale, the Sun would be as tall as a ten-story building.

TRAVELING THE SOLAR SYSTEM

If you started at the Sun and traveled outward, you could cross the paths of all eight planets in this order: Mercury, Venus, Earth, Mars, Jupiter, Saturn, Uranus, and Neptune. Mercury can reach a scorching 800°F (430°C) during the day. Neptune has an average temperature of about −390°F (−200°C).

Some people use the phrase "My Very Educated Mother Just Served Us Noodles" to remember the planets in order. Can you make up your own sentence?

THE MOON

This rocky sphere appears as the biggest and brightest object in our night sky. The Moon moves around Earth, taking about 30 days to complete one full **orbit.** The Moon is about 239,000 miles (384,000 km) away from us. If your globe and the Moon were to scale, the Moon would be the size of a small grapefruit.

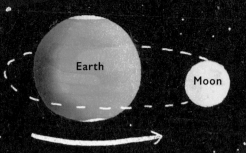

Earth

Moon

Astronauts on the International Space Station conduct experiments in astronomy, biology, physics, and other fields.

INTERNATIONAL SPACE STATION

The International Space Station is a large spacecraft that orbits Earth about 250 miles (400 km) above the surface. Traveling at approximately 17,000 miles per hour (28,000 km per hour), it makes one orbit around Earth about every 90 minutes. It is home to astronauts from many parts of the world.

BEYOND THE SOLAR SYSTEM

Our galaxy is full of stars. Most stars, like our Sun, are centers of other solar systems, with other planets or stars spinning around them. The next closest star is about 25 trillion miles (40 trillion kilometers) away! Its light takes about four years to reach Earth, so we say that it is about four **light-years** away.

9

EARTH AND THE SUN

The Sun gives us light. The way that Earth rotates on its axis and revolves around the Sun causes day and night, as well as the seasons. Using your globe, let's find out how it works!

NIGHT AND DAY

Earth is like a giant spinning ball with an imaginary line called an axis running through it. About every 24 hours, Earth makes one complete rotation around this axis. In a dark room, shine a flashlight at your globe. This represents the Sun. Half of the globe is lit, and the other half is in shadow. Spin the globe slowly and you'll see how different parts of Earth are in day or night.

THE SEASONS

Seasons are caused by Earth's tilt as it orbits the Sun. When the Northern Hemisphere is tilted toward the Sun, it is exposed to more direct sunlight and experiences spring and summer. The Southern Hemisphere, which is then tilted away from the Sun, does not get direct sunlight, and so it experiences fall and winter. The Southern Hemisphere experiences spring and summer when the Earth's tilt exposes that part of the world to direct sunlight. The Northern Hemispher then experiences fall and winter.

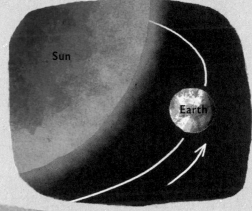

Sun

Earth

DID YOU KNOW?

The Sun never sets at the South Pole in the summer, making it light for months at a time. In winter, the Sun never rises and the land is dark.

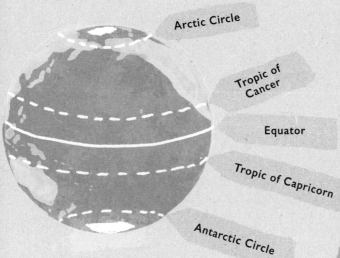

Arctic Circle

Tropic of Cancer

Equator

Tropic of Capricorn

Antarctic Circle

TIME ZONES

The world is divided into time zones to account for the fact that different parts of Earth enter and exit daylight at different times. Some large countries have several time zones. In Canada and the U.S., it could be morning in one city and afternoon in another.

IMAGINARY LINES

Your globe shows imaginary lines running around Earth. The equator runs around the middle, at Earth's widest point. It divides our planet into the Northern and Southern Hemispheres. The Tropic of Cancer and the Tropic of Capricorn lie between the equator and the poles. They mark the farthest north or south you can travel and still have the Sun directly overhead.

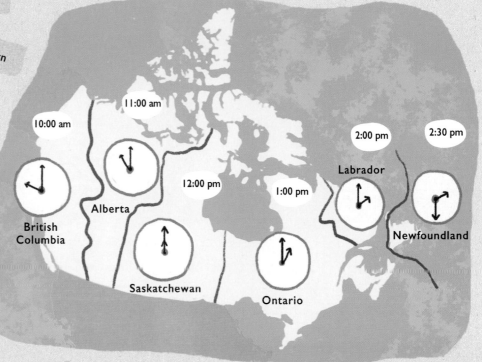

10:00 am — British Columbia
11:00 am — Alberta
12:00 pm — Saskatchewan
1:00 pm — Ontario
2:00 pm — Labrador
2:30 pm — Newfoundland

Scientists work from research stations based in Antarctica.

LAND AND WATER

Give your globe a spin and you will see how much of it is covered in water. It's no wonder Earth is known as the "blue planet"! Nearly all of this water is made up of the salt water of the oceans.

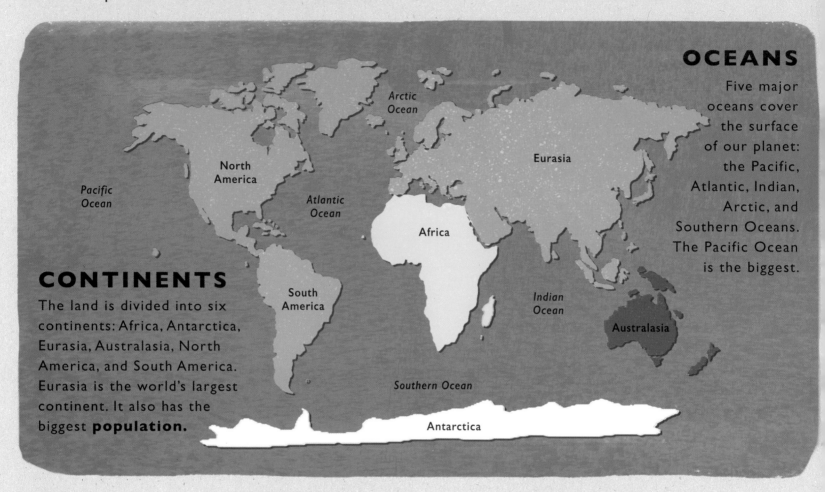

OCEANS

Five major oceans cover the surface of our planet: the Pacific, Atlantic, Indian, Arctic, and Southern Oceans. The Pacific Ocean is the biggest.

CONTINENTS

The land is divided into six continents: Africa, Antarctica, Eurasia, Australasia, North America, and South America. Eurasia is the world's largest continent. It also has the biggest **population.**

COUNTRIES

Continents are divided into smaller regions called countries, which have their own governments and where the people often share a common culture. On your globe, borders between countries are marked with a thin black line.

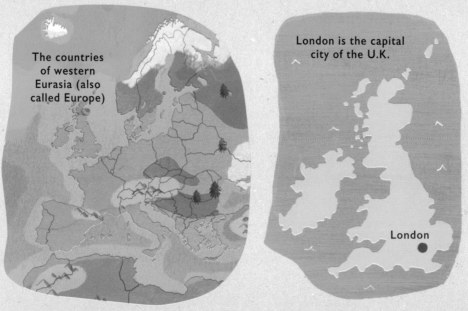

The countries of western Eurasia (also called Europe)

London is the capital city of the U.K.

London

CITIES

Countries have many cities, where large numbers of people live close together among stores, offices, and public buildings. Most major cities are found along rivers or near a coast.

LAND MEETS WATER

On the globe, the water all looks the same, but under the surface there are great differences depending on depth and distance from land. The land and ocean basin are both part of Earth's **crust.** The parts we live on are just higher than the rest.

THE GREAT BARRIER REEF

The Great Barrier Reef is a giant underwater structure made of a huge colony of animals called coral polyps. It lies off the coast of Australia, stretching across the shallow continental shelf to deeper water. It supports a wide variety of life, from cuttlefish and sea cucumbers to sharks and sponges.

Sunlight Zone — the surface of the ocean, bathed in light from the Sun. More than 90 percent of undersea life is found here.

Twilight Zone — the poorly lit part of the ocean beneath the sunlight zone. Plants do not grow here.

Midnight Zone — the completely dark, freezing ocean beneath the twilight zone. Only animals that have adapted to little light can survive here.

Continental Shelf — the shallow ocean that surrounds a continent.

Continental Slope — the steep slope where the edge of a continent falls away into the deep ocean.

Continental Rise — the boundary between a continent and the deepest part of the ocean.

Ocean Basin — the area of Earth's surface covered by an ocean.

Ocean Trench — a deep channel in the ocean floor.

BIOMES

A biome is a large region with a specific type of **climate** and distinctive plants. Biomes such as deserts are found on land. Other biomes are found in water. Each is home to different types of animals.

The Amazon is the world's largest rain forest. High up in the treetops, animals from snakes to sloths make their homes in the maze of leaves and branches.

TROPICAL RAIN FOREST

It's hot and humid in the rain forest. Tall trees form a dense **canopy** that blocks out sunlight and prevents it from reaching the forest floor. Rain forests cover just 6 percent of Earth's surface, but they are home to a huge range of different living things.

Looking at your globe, can you find the rain forest in South America?

TAIGA

The taiga is a huge forest of evergreen trees that stretches across the northernmost part of Earth's surface. It is blanketed in snow for much of the year.

Huge portions of Russia, the world's largest country, are covered in taiga. Can you find two other countries with this biome?

ICE AND SNOW

Can you imagine living in a place that's colder than the inside of your freezer? The polar regions of Earth surround the North and South Poles, and only a very few species can survive there.

The southern ice cap is on land, in Antarctica. The northern ice cap is on water. In which ocean is it located?

DESERT

Deserts receive little or no rainfall. Few animals and plants can survive in them.

The Tuareg people travel through the Sahara, the largest hot desert in the world, to trade goods. Can you find which continent the Sahara is in?

ALL THE BIOMES

These colors are used to show the different biomes on your globe. Can you find them all?

- Ocean
- Freshwater
- Tropical rain forest
- Temperate forest
- Taiga
- Savanna
- Temperate grassland
- Tundra
- Desert
- Ice and snow

FRESHWATER

Freshwater accounts for less than 3 percent of the water on Earth. It is carried from one area to another by rivers, which flow through the landscape. Along the way, rivers give life to many plants and animals.

The Nile, in Africa, is the longest river in the world. Which sea does it empty into?

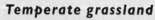

EXTREME EARTH

Earth is a planet of extremes. Earthquakes, hurricanes, and volcanoes act as powerful forces on the land and water. Where they occur can depend on climate or how the planet beneath them is formed.

VOLCANOES

A volcano is a rupture in Earth's crust, usually visible as a mountain or a hill, through which hot lava, steam, and ash shoot out. Erupting volcanoes, although spectacular, are extremely dangerous. Their effects can be felt many thousands of miles away.

The Ring of Fire is an area bordering the Pacific Ocean with many volcanoes. Can you find five countries in Asia that border the Pacific Ocean?

The island of Krakatoa (Krakatau) has one of the most active volcanoes in the world. It frequently spews out lava (molten rock), ash, and hot gases. In 1883, a series of huge explosions almost destroyed the island and killed more than 36,000 people.

TROPICAL CYCLONES

Tropical cyclones are intense, swirling storms that form over **tropical** ocean waters. Their winds can reach speeds of more than 190 miles (310 km) per hour. They include Atlantic **hurricanes,** Pacific typhoons, and Indian Ocean cyclones.

Hurricanes often occur in the Caribbean Sea. Can you find the largest island in this sea?

BUSHFIRES AND FOREST FIRES

Bushfires and forest fires are uncontrolled fires that break out in scrubland and forests when the countryside is hot and dry. Some bushfires are so big that the smoke can be seen from space.

Bushfires are common in Australia's savanna, which makes up much of what is called the Outback. Can you find it on your globe?

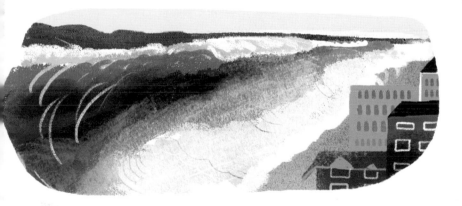

TSUNAMIS

Earthquakes occur when part of Earth's crust moves suddenly. When they happen under the ocean, they can trigger tsunamis, giant waves that can reach many feet in height. Tsunamis roll across the sea and eventually hit land, sometimes sweeping away entire towns.

Indonesia and Japan have both been hit by tsunamis in the 21st century. Which of these countries is farther south?

MONSOONS

Monsoons bring seasonal rainy periods that affect many tropical regions. People rely on the monsoon to water crops, but too much rain can flood the land and destroy homes.

Bangladesh is prone to flooding from monsoons. Which country is its largest neighbor?

NATURAL WONDERS

Earth's landscapes have been shaped by forces underground and water moving across the land. Some of these landscapes are truly spectacular! Here are some examples. Can you find more?

PAMUKKALE
TURKEY

The sparkling white rock pools at Pamukkale in Turkey are full of mineral-rich water. People swim in the **thermal springs.** Some people think that the salty water is good for their health.

Can you name four countries that border Turkey?

ULURU
AUSTRALIA

Uluru is a large rock formation rising up from the flat lands of the Australian Outback. It is sacred to the Aboriginal people of the area.

Can you name two countries near Australia?

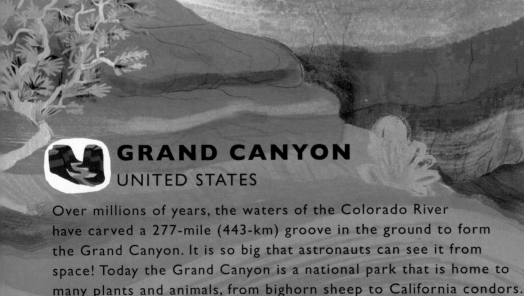

GRAND CANYON
UNITED STATES

Over millions of years, the waters of the Colorado River have carved a 277-mile (443-km) groove in the ground to form the Grand Canyon. It is so big that astronauts can see it from space! Today the Grand Canyon is a national park that is home to many plants and animals, from bighorn sheep to California condors.

Which ocean does the Colorado River flow into?

MOSI-OA-TUNYA (VICTORIA FALLS)
ZAMBIA AND ZIMBABWE

Mosi-oa-Tunya is one of the world's largest waterfalls. Every second, nearly 264,000 gallons (1,000,000 liters) of water plummets over the falls as the mighty Zambezi River flows toward the Indian Ocean.

Can you find a country that borders both Zambia and Zimbabwe?

SAGARMATHA (MOUNT EVEREST)
NEPAL

At 29,029 feet (8,848 m) high, Sagarmatha is the tallest mountain above sea level in the world. Sagarmatha is part of the Himalayas, a range that spans central Asia, from Pakistan to Bhutan.

Can you name two countries that fall within the Himalayas mountain range?

JEITA GROTTO
LEBANON

Jeita Grotto is a huge maze of underground caves and chambers. Stunning **stalactites** hang from the ceiling and **stalagmites** rise from the floor.

Which large body of water borders Lebanon?

ALL KINDS OF ANIMALS

There are millions of different types of animals in the world. Some are vertebrates, like us, with backbones inside their bodies. Others are invertebrates, with no backbones. Here are just a few examples of each.

KOMODO DRAGON

The Komodo dragon is the world's largest lizard and can grow up to 10 feet (3 m) long. Lizards are vertebrates known as reptiles, a group that also includes snakes and turtles. Reptiles are cold-blooded animals with dry, scaly skin.

The Komodo dragon lives on islands in Indonesia. Which two oceans are on either side of the islands?

PIRANHA

Piranhas live in South American rivers, where they use their razor-sharp teeth to strip the flesh from their prey. Piranhas are fish, a group of vertebrates that live and breathe in water.

The South American rain forest is spread over eight countries. Can you find two of them?

EMPEROR PENGUIN

Emperor penguins are the biggest species of penguin, and they spend their life in Antarctica. In cold weather they huddle together to keep warm. Penguins are birds — vertebrates that have feathers and lay eggs. Unlike most other birds, penguins swim rather than fly.

What is the name of the ocean that surrounds Antarctica?

GIRAFFE

The towering giraffe is the world's tallest land animal and a vertebrate. It roams the African **savanna** alongside wildebeests, elephants, and zebras, grazing on plants. All of these animals are mammals and are hunted by other mammals, such as leopards and lions.

Which big cat lives in the savanna of Angola?

CANE TOAD

EARTHWORM

GIANT OCTOPUS

Cane toads are large, warty toads from Central and South America. They are now found in many parts of the world. They belong to a group of vertebrates called amphibians, which have moist skin and lay eggs.

What is the largest country in South America?

Earthworms have a long, snake-like body and no legs. They live in soil, burrowing through it to find food. One species found in South Africa can grow many feet long! There are many other types of worms. They are all invertebrates.

Can you find two countries that border South Africa?

The giant octopus can be found in the Pacific Ocean. It has eight long arms that help it catch prey. It is a mollusk, an invertebrate with a soft, squishy body. Mollusks are found on land and at sea.

Can you find three North American countries with coastlines on the Pacific Ocean?

JAPANESE SPIDER CRAB

The Japanese spider crab has the longest legs of any crab. It lives in the oceans near Japan. It belongs to a group of invertebrates called crustaceans, which have a hard outer shell.

In which ocean is Japan located?

QUEEN ALEXANDRA'S BIRDWING

The Queen Alexandra's birdwing is the largest butterfly on Earth. Butterflies are a member of a common group of invertebrates called insects. Insects have six legs, and bodies that are divided into three parts.

The birdwing's home is in Papua New Guinea. Which large country lies to its south?

ANIMALS ON THE MOVE

Every year some animals migrate, or move from one place to another. The animals shown here take some of the longest journeys in the world. Find their icons on the globe to see where they begin their journeys, then follow their route with your finger to their journey's end.

 ## ARCTIC TERN

The Arctic tern makes the world's longest migration journey. Every year, these birds can make a round-trip of more than 43,500 miles (70,000 km) from the Arctic to Antarctica, then back again six months later. By the end of its life, an Arctic tern will have flown far enough to go around the world about sixty times!

**Antarctica is a continent.
True or false?**

Arctic terns fly over coastal towns as they begin the journey south from their nesting grounds.

Arctic terns stop to nest on beaches and feed on small fish in shallow coastal waters.

Arctic

Antarctic

LEATHERBACK SEA TURTLE

Female leatherbacks return to the same tropical beach where they were born to lay their eggs. This can mean swimming up to 12,500 miles (20,000 km)! Some swim from the West Coast of the United States to Indonesia.

Which ocean lies between Indonesia and the United States?

ATLANTIC WILD SALMON

Some Atlantic wild salmon start life in freshwater rivers in the United Kingdom. After a few years, they migrate to rich ocean feeding grounds near Greenland. Later they make the long journey back to breed in the river in which they were born.

On their journey from the United Kingdom to Greenland, the salmon must swim past which two island countries?

HUMPBACK WHALE

Each year, humpback whales swim from their feeding grounds near the poles to breeding grounds in the tropics. One group travels between Alaska and Hawaii. They can make the 3,000-mile (4,830-km) trip in as little as five weeks!

Alaska borders what country?

CARIBOU

During the short summer in northern Alaska, snow melts to reveal lush, grassy meadows. Caribou travel here to give birth. As summer ends and the snow returns, the caribou migrate back south to find food. The round-trip can be up to 1,242 miles (2,000 km) long.

Can you name another mammal that lives in Alaska?

ENDANGERED ANIMALS

Our planet is home to many remarkable creatures, but some are now very few in number due to **poaching,** habitat loss, or **global warming.** The animals on these pages are just some of those that now face a battle for survival.

Tigers use speed and stealth to hunt animals such as antelope and deer.

TIGER
ASIA

Tigers are fearsome predators with distinctive black stripes and orange-red fur. They are the biggest of all wild cats, and also some of the most endangered animals on our planet. **Fossils** show that tigers have been around for more than two million years. Today, they are in danger of **extinction** in the wild.

The tiger is the national symbol of India. Which ocean does India border?

AXOLOTL
MEXICO

This odd-looking amphibian has a lizard-like body covered in smooth, moist skin. If it loses a leg, it can grow a new one! Unlike most amphibians, axolotls spend their whole life in freshwater. They are kept as pets, but very few remain in the wild.

Using your globe, what extreme weather can you find in the Gulf of Mexico?

CALIFORNIA CONDOR
NORTH AMERICA

With a 10-foot (3-m) wingspan, the condor is the largest flying bird in North America. Condors soar high in the sky, scanning the ground for dead animals. They became extinct in the wild in 1987, but birds bred in captivity have now been released into the wild.

What mountain range spans the western United States?

EUROPEAN EEL
EUROPE

These fish were once common in European rivers, but they are now on the brink of extinction. Adults travel across the Atlantic Ocean to lay their eggs. The young eels drift back to Europe to grow up before returning to the sea where they were born.

Which European country is the farthest southwest?

LORD HOWE ISLAND STICK INSECT
AUSTRALIA

Stick insects live all over the world, but the Lord Howe Island stick insect is only found on a few tiny islands in Australia. When rats arrived on the islands about 100 years ago, they hunted the stick insects. Scientists found a few survivors and are breeding them.

Which ocean lies off the east coast of Australia?

GHARIAL
SOUTH ASIA

The gharial has a long, slender snout lined with rows of sharp teeth. Gharials live in the fast-flowing rivers of South Asia, where they snap up small fish and other animals. Only a few hundred gharials are left in the wild.

Some gharials live in Nepal. Which two countries border Nepal?

25

WORLD HERITAGE

Throughout history, humans have left their mark on the landscape. Some of the most amazing landmarks are protected as World Heritage Sites. These buildings and structures help tell the story of human history.

GREAT WALL OF CHINA
CHINA

The Great Wall of China is an enormous brick and stone **barricade** that stretches for about 13,170 miles (22,000 km). Construction started more than 2,000 years ago and took more than 1,000 years to complete.

Can you name a country that lies to the north of China?

A large portion of the wall has disappeared. Most of the remaining sections are between 400 and 600 years old.

STONEHENGE
UNITED KINGDOM

Stonehenge is a circle of huge standing stones on a flat plain in the United Kingdom. No one really knows who built it or what it was used for.

Which continent is the United Kingdom a part of?

 # GREAT PYRAMID
EGYPT

The Great Pyramid at Giza was built from more than two million large limestone blocks. It was the tomb of the **pharaoh** Khufu.

Egypt has coastlines along which two seas?

 # COLOSSEUM
ITALY

The massive Colosseum was built by the ancient Romans. It was an arena where more than 50,000 spectators could watch **gladiator** fights, **chariot** races, and even mock sea battles.

The Colosseum is in Rome, the capital of Italy. Which continent lies directly south?

 # TAJ MAHAL
INDIA

This marble building in Agra, India, was commissioned by Emperor Shah Jahan to house the tomb of his favorite wife, Mumtaz Mahal.

Can you name the two seas near India?

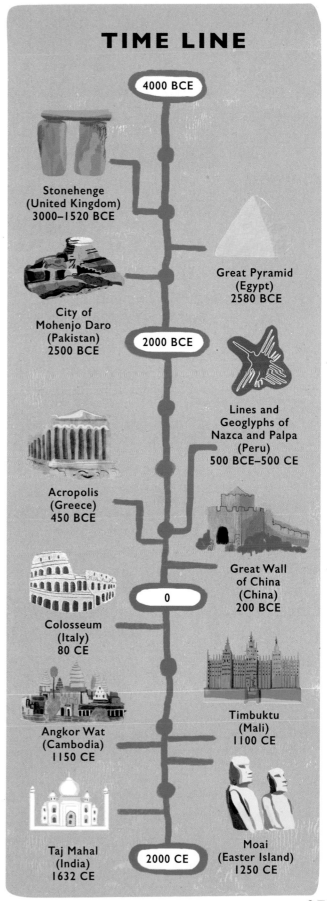

TIME LINE

4000 BCE

Stonehenge
(United Kingdom)
3000–1520 BCE

Great Pyramid
(Egypt)
2580 BCE

City of
Mohenjo Daro
(Pakistan)
2500 BCE

2000 BCE

Lines and
Geoglyphs of
Nazca and Palpa
(Peru)
500 BCE–500 CE

Acropolis
(Greece)
450 BCE

Great Wall
of China
(China)
200 BCE

0

Colosseum
(Italy)
80 CE

Great Wall
of China
(China)
200 BCE

Angkor Wat
(Cambodia)
1150 CE

Timbuktu
(Mali)
1100 CE

Taj Mahal
(India)
1632 CE

2000 CE

Moai
(Easter Island)
1250 CE

MEGACITIES

More than half of the world's people live in cities. Some of these sprawling settlements have turned into "megacities" — cities that are home to 10 million people or more. Here are six of them.

SHANGHAI
CHINA

Shanghai is the biggest city in China, with buildings ranging from traditional Chinese homes to some of the tallest skyscrapers in the world.

Which ocean does the port of Shanghai sit in?

LONDON
UNITED KINGDOM

London has a long history that dates back to Roman times. Today, it is one of the world's most popular tourist destinations.

Which sea separates the United Kingdom from Denmark?

NEW YORK
UNITED STATES

New York is a city of skyscrapers, sidewalks, and yellow taxicabs. It is incredibly diverse because people from many countries around the world have made it their home. Well-known landmarks include the Statue of Liberty, the Empire State Building, and Times Square.

Which ocean would you have to cross to reach London sailing from New York?

LAGOS
NIGERIA

Lagos is the largest city of Nigeria and the African continent and is known across Africa as a center of culture, with open-air music festivals and a thriving movie industry known as "Nollywood."

On which ocean is Nigeria's coastline?

MEXICO CITY
MEXICO

Mexico City is at a high altitude and surrounded by mountains and volcanoes. It was founded by the Aztecs in 1325 as Tenochtitlán.

Can you find a country that borders Mexico to the south?

TOKYO
JAPAN

Tokyo has more people than any other city. Famous for its modern buildings and neon-lit streets, it is also steeped in centuries of culture and tradition.

Can you name four countries that border the Sea of Japan?

New York City is the most densely populated city in the United States.

UNUSUAL JOBS

People have jobs in all kinds of different places. Some jobs are linked to an area's landscape or weather. Here are a few of the world's most unusual jobs!

ICE SCULPTOR
CHINA

Using chisels, handsaws, and even chainsaws, these artists carve frozen masterpieces from solid blocks of ice. Harbin, China, hosts an annual festival where enormous ice sculptures are displayed.

China is located on which continent?

ICEBERG MOVER
NORTH ATLANTIC OCEAN

Iceberg movers work to prevent ships from colliding with icebergs. They use **satellites** and **radar** to locate giant chunks of ice, then use tugboats to tow them away from busy shipping lanes.

Which of these islands in the North Atlantic is larger: Iceland or Greenland?

PEARL DIVER
JAPAN

Beautiful pearls grow inside **oysters,** which live deep in the world's oceans. Japanese pearl divers often collect the oysters by free diving down into the water, holding their breath for minutes at a time.

Can you name a giant invertebrate found living near Japan's coast?

SNAKE MILKER
THAILAND

Thailand is in the tropics — the perfect habitat for many snakes. Snake milkers extract venom from dangerous snakes. Doctors need it to produce **antivenin,** the best way of treating snakebites.

Can you name two countries that border Thailand?

SNOWMAKER
CANADA

Snowmakers at ski resorts such as Canmore in Alberta, Canada, keep the slopes supplied with snow. They use snowmaking machines to cover the slopes with perfect powdery snow.

What is the only country that borders Canada?

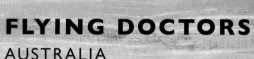

FLYING DOCTORS
AUSTRALIA

If you think flying airplanes and saving people's lives sounds like fun, then the Australian Royal Flying Doctor Service might be for you. These doctors provide emergency medical care in some of the most remote places in Australia. Their planes carry patients back to city hospitals for treatment.

Can you name two biomes that are found in Australia?

The Flying Doctors made their first flight in 1928.

TRAVELING THE WORLD

The ability to travel by land, sea, and air has allowed people and ideas to spread around the globe.

 ## IN THE AIR

A trip on a passenger jet is the quickest way to travel long distances. At some airports, tens of millions of passengers arrive and depart each year. At busy times, an airplane takes off or lands every minute somewhere in the world.

The world's busiest airport is in the United States, in Atlanta, Georgia. What biome is Atlanta in?

An Airbus A320 waits for a signal to go to the runway for take-off at Atlanta's busy airport.

UNDER THE CITY

Subway systems avoid busy streets by using underground tunnels. Some carry millions of passengers every day.

Beijing, China, has one of the busiest subway systems. Can you name two rivers found in China?

IN THE CITY

City centers can be crowded with cars and buses. In some cities, motorized tuk-tuks are a quicker way to travel. They originate from passenger carts called rickshaws, which were pulled by hand.

Tuk-tuks are common in Bangkok, Thailand. On which continent will you find Thailand?

CROSSING CONTINENTS

Before airplanes, trains were the fastest way for people to travel long distances. The Trans-Siberian Railway, which crosses Russia, is the world's longest passenger railroad line. It takes a week to travel the entire 6,000-mile (9,000-km) railway.

Can you name two biomes that the Trans-Siberian Railway passes through?

ACROSS OCEANS

Ocean cruises are a favorite way for many people to get from one place to another. Some cruise ships travel through the Panama Canal. The 50-mile (80-km) canal trip is shorter than a 9,200-mile (14,800-km) journey around South America.

Can you name a country that borders Panama?

33

FAMOUS FACES

Many people have shaped history, from scientists and artists to politicians and writers. This gallery of famous faces highlights some of those whose influence is still felt today.

Actors perform one of Shakespeare's plays for an audience at the Globe Theatre in London.

WILLIAM SHAKESPEARE

UNITED KINGDOM

William Shakespeare is one of the most famous writers of all time. Born in 1564, he wrote 38 plays as well as many poems. In the hundreds of years since his death, his works have been translated into many languages and performed all over the world.

Which sea lies to the east of the United Kingdom?

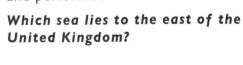

MAHATMA GANDHI
INDIA

Political activist Mahatma Gandhi led India to independence from the United Kingdom. He promoted peaceful protest and campaigned on behalf of the poor. India became independent in 1947, but was split into two countries — India and Pakistan. Mahatma Gandhi has inspired civil rights movements around the world.

Which famous mountain is in Nepal, to the north of India?

AMELIA EARHART
UNITED STATES

In 1932, Amelia Earhart became the first woman to fly solo nonstop across the Atlantic Ocean. She was a daring adventurer as well as an advocate for women's causes. In 1937, Earhart disappeared while attempting a round-the-world flight.

On her final flight, Earhart took off from Papua New Guinea. Which islands lie directly to the east of Papua New Guinea?

LEO TOLSTOY
RUSSIA

Leo Tolstoy is best known for his classic novel *War and Peace,* which tells the story of Russian life during the Napoleonic Wars in the early 19th century. Tolstoy wrote throughout his long life, inspiring generations of novelists who followed him.

Which continent is Russia on?

NELSON MANDELA
SOUTH AFRICA

Nelson Mandela was a political activist who was influential in ending **apartheid** in South Africa. He became the first black president of South Africa in 1994 and has inspired human rights movements throughout the world.

Which country lies completely within the borders of the country of South Africa?

ABRAHAM LINCOLN
UNITED STATES

Abraham Lincoln was a president of the United States. He led the country through a civil war. Lincoln also helped to end American slavery by issuing the Emancipation Proclamation and supporting the passage of the 13th Amendment to the U.S. Constitution.

Which lakes form part of the border between the United States and Canada?

FRIDA KAHLO
MEXICO

Frida Kahlo was a 20th century painter whose works explore facets of Mexican society such as identity and class. Her unique style is also one of the most recognizable.

Mexico lies on which continent?

SALVADOR DALÍ
SPAIN

Salvador Dalí was an artist known for painting in a dream-like style called **surrealism.** His paintings show things like melting clocks and elephants on stilts. Dalí's eccentric behavior shocked people, but he was one of the most influential artists of the 20th century.

Which sea lies to the southeast of Spain?

ALBERT EINSTEIN
GERMANY/USA/ SWITZERLAND

Albert Einstein was a scientist who changed the way we view the universe by helping to develop modern physics. Born in Germany in 1879, he was once called "an unremarkable student," but he is now celebrated for his groundbreaking scientific work.

True or false: Germany shares a border with Russia.

MARIE CURIE
POLAND/FRANCE

Marie Curie discovered two elements, polonium and radium, with Pierre Curie. She was the first woman to win a Nobel Prize, the first person and only woman to win the prize twice, and the only person to win a Nobel Prize in two different sciences (chemistry and physics).

Which country has borders with both France and Poland?

35

SPORTS ZONE

Sports are played and watched by millions of people around the world. Here is a selection of different sports, many of which can be seen all over the world.

SUMO WRESTLING
JAPAN

Sumo wrestling goes back at least 2,000 years. Each wrestler tries to throw his opponent out of the ring or knock him off his feet.

Is Japan in the Northern or Southern Hemisphere?

SURFING
AUSTRALIA

Surfing started in Polynesian culture. Surfers stand on a board and ride the surface of a wave as it crashes into the shore. Australia is home to some of the world's most famous surfing beaches.

Australia is surrounded by which oceans?

CYCLING
FRANCE

Cycling is popular worldwide, but every year the world's best road cyclists compete in a long, grueling race across France, known as the Tour de France. The leader after each daily "stage" earns the right to wear the famous yellow jersey.

Which country borders France to the southwest?

DOWNHILL SKIING
NORWAY

Skiing started as a way to travel, but it became a sport in 19th-century Norway. Races soon became popular throughout Europe. Downhill skiing now exists all over the world; for example, there are well-known slopes in Chile and Argentina.

Which sea lies to the north of Norway?

SOCCER
GHANA

Various soccer-like games have been played throughout history, but the modern sport originated in the United Kingdom. Today it is one of the most popular sports in the world and is the most popular sport in Ghana.

Ghana is located between which two countries?

AUTO RACING
FRANCE

Since 1923, the city of Le Mans in France has hosted the world's oldest sports car endurance race. Teams of drivers take turns speeding around the Circuit de la Sarthe at hundreds of miles per hour.

Which sea is south of France?

During the Tour de France, the best climber wears the polka-dot jersey and the fastest sprinter wears a green jersey.

ARTS AND MUSIC

Humans have been making art and music since prehistoric times. These art forms are important ways for people from different cultures to tell their stories.

The Carnival in Rio de Janeiro draws millions of people.

CARNIVAL
BRAZIL

Carnival marks the beginning of the Christian tradition of **Lent** each year. It is a time of celebration when processions with floats and brass bands dance and march through the streets. Rio de Janeiro, Brazil, is the world's Carnival capital! Visitors watch the **samba** dancers in their colorful costumes.

Which ocean is located to the east of Brazil?

CALLIGRAPHY
CHINA

Calligraphy is the art of decorative handwriting. It has been practiced for thousands of years in China, where artists use ink to make the symbols used in Chinese writing. It takes years to master the delicate brushstrokes.

Which ocean lies off the east coast of China?

 ## BALLET
RUSSIA

Ballet is a graceful and precise form of dance. It began in Italy in the 1500s, then spread throughout Europe and eventually the world. Today, Russia's Bolshoi Ballet is one of the world's most famous ballet companies.

Which famous railway line runs across Russia?

 ## PANPIPES
PERU

Traditional panpipes consist of a series of pipes of different lengths. The pipes are bound together and each plays a different note. A performer blows across the ends of the pipes to make music.

Can you name two countries that border Peru?

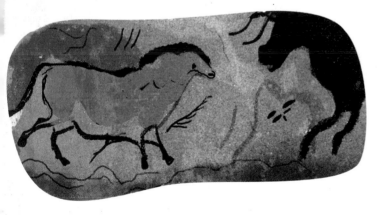

CAVE PAINTINGS
FRANCE

Cave paintings are some of the world's oldest works of art. The paintings on cave walls in Lascaux, France, are more than 17,000 years old. They show human figures and animals.

Can you name the famous tower in the center of Paris?

FABULOUS FOOD

Most foods are associated with particular countries. Take a look at this menu of dishes from around the world, from spicy Indian curries to American barbecue and hamburgers.

 ## BEEF
ARGENTINA

Argentina is a country of beef producers where farmers graze their cattle on the fertile grasslands. Beef is cooked over a charcoal flame and served with other grilled meats and a sauce called chimichurri.

Which long, narrow country borders Argentina to the west?

PIZZA
ITALY

Pizza is now eaten all over the world, but it originated in Italy centuries ago, when people added cheese, garlic, and salt to flatbread.

Can you name two European countries that share a border with Italy?

TAPAS
SPAIN

Barcelona, Spain, is home to La Boqueria — one of Europe's biggest, oldest, and busiest food markets. From lunchtime through the evening, hungry shoppers eat tapas, small dishes of food, at special tapas bars.

Spain is closest to which country in Africa?

HAMBURGERS
UNITED STATES

American food ranges from spicy **Cajun** cooking to sweet, sticky barbecue. But few foods have become as popular around the world as the hamburger!

Cajun cooking originated in the state of Louisiana. What gulf is closest to the southern U.S.?

CURRY
INDIA

A curry is a dish flavored with fragrant herbs, chilies, and tasty spices such as cumin, coriander, and turmeric. Curries are often eaten with steamed rice or bread.

Which island nation lies just off India's southern tip?

TACOS
MEXICO

Mexican food is ancient and complex and often includes tomatoes, chili peppers, corn, cocoa, and avocados. Tacos consist of tortillas and a variety of fillings and are popular in Mexico and throughout the world.

Which body of water borders Mexico's western coast and Baja California?

At La Boqueria you can buy many different varieties of specialty Spanish ham and fresh fruits and vegetables.

41

CAN YOU FIND THEM?

You'll find all of the icons from this book on your globe, as well as many more. See if you can spot them all! To learn more about the icons shown here, ask a parent or teacher to help you look them up online or at the library.

NORTH AMERICA

quetzal · maple syrup · Tikal · bald eagle · Route 66 · Palacio de Bellas Artes

Statue of Liberty · taxi · Canada goose · sugar skull · snowy owl · White House

SOUTH AMERICA

Galápagos tortoise · Machu Picchu · tango dancers · Nazca Lines · stilt house · Christ the Redeemer

panpipes · anaconda · parrot · flamingo · Tungurahua Volcano · jaguar

EUROPE

 Guggenheim Museum

 St. Basil's Cathedral

 pretzel

 bagpipes

 Fair Isle sweater

 Eiffel Tower

 Gamla Stan

 Hagia Sophia

 accordion

 ancient Greek temple

 red deer

 Santorini

 Sagrada Família

 European eel

 St. Sophia's Cathedral

 puffin

 Norwegian Folk Museum

 marmot

AFRICA

 black rhino

 buffalo

 tagine dish

 souks

 Aswan Dam

 Sphinx

 National Arts Theatre

 djembe drum

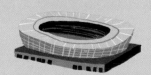 Cape Town Stadium

 mbira

 secretary bird

 woven basket

43

CAN YOU FIND THEM?

ASIA

pomegranate

tarsier

Bayterek Tower

giant panda

rocket

subway

bento

Oriental Pearl Tower

Bohol Chocolate Hills

Burj Al Arab

table tennis

oud

Mohenjo-daro

Indian elephant

Maimun Palace

Buddha statue

matryoshka doll

Shah-i-Zinda

Indian classical dance

Grand Mosque

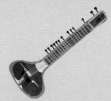
Xinjiang hat

sitar

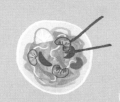
tae kwon do

pad Thai

pangolin

Chinese dragon

snow leopard

yak

monkey

Persian rug

AUSTRALASIA

Sydney Opera House

Wai-O-Tapu Thermal Wonderland

Aboriginal art

Sri Siva Subramaniya temple

State Library Victoria

kiwi

emu

the Beehive

didgeridoo

koala

boomerang

opal

ANTARCTICA

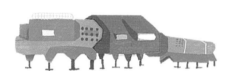
Halley Research Station

Antarctic shag

leopard seal

Weddell seal

Amundsen-Scott South Pole Station

OCEANS

sperm whale

Portuguese man-of-war

angelfish

sailfish

giant squid

clownfish

sunfish

tuna

coral

dugong

narwhal

Arctic char

ANSWERS

pp. 14–15: **Biomes**
Taiga: *possible answers are Sweden, Finland, Norway, Canada, United States, Kazakhstan, Mongolia, China*
Ice and Snow: *Arctic Ocean*
Desert: *Africa*
Freshwater: *Mediterranean Sea*

pp. 16–17: **Extreme Earth**
Volcanoes: *possible answers are Russia, Japan, North Korea, South Korea, China, Taiwan, Philippines, Vietnam, Indonesia*
Tropical Cyclones: *Cuba*
Tsunamis: *Indonesia*
Monsoons: *India*

pp. 18–19: **Natural Wonders**
Pamukkale: *possible answers are Syria, Greece, Bulgaria, Georgia, Armenia, Iraq, Iran*
Uluru: *possible answers are New Zealand and Papua New Guinea*
Grand Canyon: *Pacific Ocean*
Mosi-Oa-Tunya: *Botswana or Mozambique*
Sagarmatha: *possible answers are Nepal, Bhutan, India, Pakistan, China*
Jeita Grotto: *Mediterranean Sea*

pp. 20–21: **All Kinds of Animals**
Komodo Dragon: *Indian Ocean, Pacific Ocean*
Piranha: *possible answers are Colombia, Venezuela, Guyana, Suriname, French Guiana, Ecuador, Peru, Bolivia, Brazil*
Emperor Penguin: *Southern Ocean*
Giraffe: *lion*
Cane Toad: *Brazil*
Earthworm: *possible answers are Namibia, Botswana, Lesotho, Swaziland, Zimbabwe, Mozambique*
Giant Octopus: *possible answers are United States, Canada, Mexico, Guatemala, El Salvador, Honduras, Nicaragua, Costa Rica, Panama*
Japanese Spider Crab: *Pacific Ocean*
Queen Alexandra's Birdwing: *Australia*

pp. 22–23: **Animals on the Move**
Arctic Tern: *true*
Leatherback Sea Turtle: *Pacific Ocean*
Atlantic Wild Salmon: *Iceland, Ireland*
Humpback Whale: *Canada*
Caribou: *possible answer is Wolf*

pp. 24–25: **Endangered Animals**
Tiger: *Indian Ocean*
Axolotl: *Tropical cyclones, hurricanes*
California Condor: *Rocky Mountains*
Lord Howe Island Stick Insect: *Pacific Ocean*
European Eel: *Portugal*
Gharial: *China, India*

pp. 26–27: **World Heritage**
Great Wall of China: *possible answers are Kyrgyzstan, Mongolia, Kazakhstan, Russia*
Stonehenge: *Eurasia*
Great Pyramid: *Mediterranean Sea, Red Sea*
Colosseum: *Africa*
Taj Mahal: *Arabian Sea and Andaman Sea*

pp. 28–29: **Megacities**
Shanghai: *Pacific Ocean*
New York: *Atlantic Ocean*
London: *North Sea*
Lagos: *Atlantic Ocean*
Mexico City: *Guatemala or Belize*
Tokyo: *Japan, North Korea, South Korea, Russia*

pp. 30–31: **Unusual Jobs**
Ice Sculptor: *Eurasia*
Iceberg Mover: *Greenland*
Snake Milker: *possible answers are Myanmar, Malaysia, Cambodia, Laos*
Pearl Diver: *giant octopus or Japanese spider crab*
Snowmaker: *United States*
Flying Doctors: *possible answers are savanna, temperate grassland, desert, temperate forest, tropical rain forest*

pp. 32–33: **Traveling the World**
In the Air: *temperate forest*
Under the City: *possible answer is Huang He River and Yangtze River*
In the City: *Eurasia*
Across Oceans: *Colombia or Costa Rica*
Crossing Continents: *taiga, temperate forest*

pp. 34–35: **Famous Faces**
William Shakespeare: *North Sea*
Mahatma Gandhi: *Sagarmatha (Mount Everest)*
Amelia Earhart: *Solomon Islands*
Leo Tolstoy: *Eurasia*
Nelson Mandela: *Lesotho*
Abraham Lincoln: *the Great Lakes*
Frida Kahlo: *North America*
Salvador Dalí: *Mediterranean Sea*
Albert Einstein: *false*
Marie Curie: *Germany*

pp. 36–37: **Sports Zone**
Surfing: *Indian Ocean and Pacific Ocean*
Sumo Wrestling: *Northern Hemisphere*
Cycling: *Spain*
Soccer: *Côte d'Ivoire and Togo*
Downhill Skiing: *Barents Sea*
Auto Racing: *Mediterranean Sea*

pp. 38–39: **Arts and Music**
Carnival: *Atlantic Ocean*
Calligraphy: *Pacific Ocean*
Ballet: *Trans-Siberian Railway*
Panpipes: *possible answers are Chile, Bolivia, Ecuador, Brazil, Colombia*
Cave Paintings: *Eiffel Tower*

pp. 40–41: **Fabulous Food**
Beef: *Chile*
Pizza: *possible answers are France, Switzerland, Croatia, Slovenia, Austria*
Tapas: *Morocco*
Hamburgers: *Gulf of Mexico*
Curry: *Sri Lanka*
Tacos: *Gulf of California*

GLOSSARY

antivenin drug for treating bites from venomous animals such as snakes

apartheid a policy or system of segregation based on race

asteroid small rocky object orbiting the Sun

barricade barrier to keep people from passing through

Cajun group of people descended from French settlers in Louisiana

canopy uppermost branches of trees in a forest

chariot horse-drawn carriage used for racing and war in ancient times

climate the general weather conditions in a particular area over a long period of time

crust the outermost layer of Earth, which is hard and rocky

earthquake violent shaking of the ground caused by movements deep within Earth

extinction when the last member of a species dies out

fossil remains of an animal or plant that lived millions of years ago, preserved in rock or another substance

gladiator person who fought in public for entertainment in ancient Rome

global warming gradual increase in the temperature of Earth's atmosphere

hurricane violent tropical storm with strong winds and heavy rain

Lent forty-day period before Easter, which Christians mark by fasting

light-year distance that light travels in one year

meteor a rocky body burning up in Earth's atmosphere, causing a bright trail in the sky

orbit path of an object around a star or planet

oyster hard-shelled mollusk that lives in salt water

pharaoh ruler in ancient Egypt

poaching illegal hunting of wild animals

population all the people who live in a specific place

radar (short for RAdio Detection And Ranging) using radio waves to locate objects

radiation energy in the form of waves or rays

samba Brazilian dance of African origin

satellite artificial object launched into space for communication or to collect information

savanna grassland in tropical and subtropical regions

stalactite structure hanging from the ceiling of a cave

stalagmite structure rising from the floor of a cave

surrealism an art movement that seeks to generate fantastic effects by using unusual combinations

thermal spring spring of naturally hot water

tropical relating to the region between the tropics of Cancer and Capricorn

INDEX